AF576774

SNOW COUNTRY

SNOW COUNTRY

Robert Hedin

COPPER CANYON PRESS 1975

ACKNOWLEDGEMENT:
Some of these poems appeared in:

Wascana Review
Raven
The Fiddlehead
The Malahat Review
Prism International
The Southern Poetry Review
Charas
Seal's Cry
The Beloit Poetry Journal
Three Rivers Poetry Journal
Beggar's Bowl
Dacotah Territory
Copperhead
Twelve Poems

Library of Congress Cataloging in Publication Data

Hedin, Robert.

Snow country.

Poems.
I. Title.
PS3558.E318S6 811'.5'4 75-2278
ISBN 0-914742-06-X

Copper Canyon Press
Box 271
Port Townsend, Washington 98368

CONTENTS

7 End
8 The Snow Country
9 Photo: White Pass Trail, 1899
10 Wind
11 Fragments
12 Owls
13 White-Out
14 Homesteading Near the Brooks Range
15 Glimpse into a Private Road
16 At the Edge of Wood Road
17 The Bees
19 Arctic Stone
20 Dream
21 Strawberry Picking
22 Last Poet
23 Sitka
24 Beached
25 Immigrant of Tansy Valley
26 Great Bear
27 At the Backwaters
28 Salmon Point
29 Snow-Clouds
30 Frankenstein
31 Goddard Hot Springs
32 Transcanadian
33 The Casca
34 Eclipse
36 Hart Crane Along the Mississippi
37 Hermitage
38 Mountain Ash
39 Harbor at Midnight
40 And the Mountains Behind
41 Sitka Spruce
43 Isadora
45 Watching Valentino
46 Instinct
48 Umbra

for Carolyn and Mother
and in memory of my father

END

At the end of the open road we come to ourselves

Louis Simpson

All right, Louis
we're here
we're here at the end of the open road
at the end of our ellipsis,
in the tail of the swan's gullet.

We stand alone.
a wind and slight drizzle hide
any other footprints.
they curl the road
around our feet,
sweeping it back into itself.

Louis, before us still lies the darkness.
in it we think
we see trees, giant sequoias
that break around an open marsh,
and are compelled to give them green
to give them sway
a hard mossy bark,
rain dripping from their leaves.

Listen. a bullfrog's call.
smell the moist calm in the air.

We wait for the moon
for the song of a white bird

Any backdrop
of light.

THE SNOW COUNTRY

Up on Verstovia the snow country is silent tonight.
I can see it from our window,
A white sea whose tide flattens over the darkness.
This is where the animals must go--
The old foxes, the bears too slow to catch
The fall run of salmon, even the salmon themselves--
All brought together in the snow country of Verstovia.
This must be where the ravens turn to geese,
The weasels to wolves, where the rabbits turn to owls.
I wonder if birds even nest on that floating sea,
What hunters have forgotten their trails and sunk out of sight.
I wonder if the snow country is green underneath,
If there are forests and paths
And cabins with wood-burning stoves.
Or does it move down silently gyrating forever,
Glistening with the bones of animals and trappers,
Eggs that are cold and turning to stones.
I wonder if I should turn, tap and even wake you.

PHOTO: WHITE PASS TRAIL, 1899

In this photo the upper third
Is so faded it looks like fog.
Notice the fine line of spruce
Leaning toward exposure,
That small wall of dirt with roots
Shooting through its bedrock.
The rest is a stock pile of mules
So bloated they look like cows.
Some remain only as haunches,
Some as ears swelled-up like leaves.
And still others are there full-blown
So you see every stalled ripple.
To the right where the fog drops off
There are some passing for boulders,
Some you could even stand on
And stare past the fog into a clearing,
And hear the voices of miners fading North,
The bray of animals, the echoes
Of stones piling up to stake a claim.
Now let your eyes fall back
Over the pile until you reach
A bleached missing piece,
Part of the puzzle someone
Has stolen as a practical joke.

WIND

Out there, where frontiers end, roads are erased

Octavio Paz

And the wind is used
Instead--
The same wind
That runs in packs

And stores the carcasses
Of horses
In its cellars

That is always taking
You down
In its arms,
And making you heavy
With its words.

And always
When roads are erased,
The wind wades
Straight into itself

Is always white,
And its moon is a great ox
Whose hooves
Are frosted with winter.

FRAGMENTS

As the moon spreads
Its light
Across the open field

It stirs from the snow
A continent
Of dark cellars.

Entering their cold
Secrets I begin
To unearth the small

Fragments of myself:
Stone bowls and axes,
Beaked ladles

Spearheads chipped
From the skulls
Of gods.

I press close
To the bedrock and feel
A colony of faces

Blurred by roots and shells,
Their mouths open
Begging for darkness.

OWLS

Owls glide off the thin
Wrists of the night,
And using snow for their feathers
Drift down on either side
Of the wind.

I always spot them
As I camp along the ridge,
Glistening over the streambeds
Their eyes small rooms
Lit by stone lamps.

WHITE-OUT

Here on this ridge all is so white
It all seems dark.
The only color left is my wife,
And soon she too will fade.
The spruce have long returned to birch;
The birch are turning to snow.
And all those green shadows
That flowed down over the road
Into warm burnt valleys and river beds--
All have burst and now lie naked.
I hear the bushes in the ditch
Crouch and paw at the white.
The stones under my feet
Are struggling to rise into swans.
Far off I hear the strike of a match.
And I see my wife's hand open
Stroking a growing white flame.

HOMESTEADING NEAR THE BROOKS RANGE

Against the hillside,
The wind rises
And drives
Through the walls

Scattering ashes over
My shadow in the window.

Far below, you rub
Your clothing in the creek;
Water gently bends
Around your breasts.

Over the stone ridge
I see your figure approach

Drawing me back
To the fire,
As your darkness
Spreads thin the coals.

GLIMPSE INTO A PRIVATE ROAD

From around the ruts
The darkness flows,
And spills itself
Into the blue
Of unpicked berries.

It rises slowly
Over the fireweed,
Through lilacs
And swollen elders,
Sliding upward until
It breaks over the crest
Of the pines;

Leaving only the brittle
Shell of a mouse,
Harboring the moon's
Light like a pearl.

AT THE EDGE OF WOOD ROAD

There's a pool deep like your eyes:
Cupped in brown willows, and shaded green
With spruce that spill down from the hills,
This pool lies still and never blinks.
On its surface there is no softness.
(All softness now lies with the moss.)
Off in a far corner where a piece of sun
Wedges itself under a ledge of bedrock,
I see glowing on the bottom
The sheered flushed ribs of a fish.
Grains of sand bounce through its bones,
Juggled by the hands of a spring.

the bees

to fred hollaus, beekeeper

someone has rattled
a giant pod and left
the sorrel and

silverweed stiff
the goldenrod white
the briar rose still

we walk out
into this dull cell
this mausoleum world where

yesterday we were
hooded and gloved
in cheesecloth

timid lords
surrounded by the whirr
of our bees

we felt the flowers
jiggle and lighten
each swollen path plunge

back into the box
back into the waxy
swarming pulse

now as we lift off
this hatch and stare
into the thousands

of milky crypts
into the hordes of limp drones
and unconscious stingers

we are bare-handed
orderlies
from another world

we reach and pick
from the brittle mass
our dazed queen

her body curled
one feeler twitching
the other broken

we cup her stir
her feeble buzz
then pause

and raise her high
opening our hands
to the crisp white air

ARCTIC STONE

Let others find root
In the curvature
Of Roman noses,
The sculptured loins
Of Greek messengers;

I will choose
The arctic stone,
A grey seed
That sings of stillness
And the divinity of fur.

Its walls preserve
Worlds of dull icy light,
Of campfires
And tribes scattered
Across the Bering.

Around the darkness
Of its core,
Fishermen huddle
And hone their spears
Against the cold;

Huts rise like hummocks,
And the shadows
Worn from human shape
Harden and become grey
Translations of their bodies.

DREAM

I dreamed the rain slid
From this island in patches,
That the forest collapsed
Into a field of cones.
I dreamed the night unhitched
Itself from its stem,
And the stars were the eyes
Of animals straying down
To graze on our lawn.
I dreamed a kingfisher
Nested at your feet,
That your hands splashed
Nakedly through Chopin.
There were mushrooms flaring
From the eaves of the piano,
And I dreamed your palms
Held a clue why the keys
Were bone and hollow with wind.

STRAWBERRY PICKING

O how Bruegel would love the way we stoop
How we soak our hands into the deep green
And trace along through the cool wet shade
As if searching for something lost
O how Bruegel would love the way we stoop
How we pick directly from these plants
And cradle only the most inflated ones
O how Bruegel would love the way we stoop
The way we wait--wanting to dip our hands
Into paraffin to preserve their royal stain

LAST POET

This man is a lover
Of canyon walls.
The first to read by moon alone.

During the day
He lives away from the sun,
Prone in the cool dirt
Under ledges
Revising that one long last narrative line
On sheets of mica.

Now is the time
He chooses his closest friends:
A cricket who's run out of songs,
A jagged piece of rock
Termed muse.

Near evening
He makes his way to a precipice
And scours
The stones for scratches
Other than his own.

And as the moon curls over the rim
He recites his work
From memory,
Then listens as the canyon reads back
Again and again.
And then he claps
And the whole canyon applauds.

SITKA

The rain is so quiet here,
So faint and so barely visible,
So clear you can watch the mountains
Rise and smolder with fog,
So quiet only the taut thick leaves
Of the skunk flower drum a sound,
So plain you can catch the gulls
Sliding out over the Pacific
Searching for trawlers,
So still they mistake the drops
For bugs just hatching,
Just flickering on the water.

BEACHED

Sitka has slid into the sea.
Left are ridges of snow--
And us
Alone on this island
With colonies of mollusks.

This is the first beach we have seen;
Its skin is warm and deep,
Wet with tides,
And rimmed by spruce
Smooth as the backs of horses.

I sit here on the rocks
And watch you wading to greet
The sea-people,
Your breasts beneath the waves
White with winter.

IMMIGRANT OF TANSY VALLEY

tansy: a strong smelling plant;
from the Greek athanasia, *immortality*

Each night after returning
From the factory, he walked
The path to the edge of the field;
Leaning over the barbs
He carefully picked a leaf
From the clump, rolled it
Like a cigarette and
Tucked it in his nostril.

Breathing the mint on the way
Back to the house, he smiled
And whispered his stories
Of the Ayrshire straits.

And as we climbed the backsteps,
He placed his hand on my shoulder
And wanted me to assure him
The tansy would never be moved,
Would be left beside the fence
For the others in the valley.

GREAT BEAR

I always see him rolling
Slowly on his side,
Always drifting
Downwind with the moon--
A bank of soft darkness,
An old weathered dirigible
Floating low over the spruce
Toward the distant muskegs
Where the milkweed
Burst like lights on a wet
Deserted airstrip.

AT THE BACKWATERS

Far beyond reach,
Near the sun's last light
Smoldering
In the bleached rush

You hunt quartz
And skitter
The nameless stones
Into the slough's reflection.

You know nothing
Of the voices
From the main channel.

Their drone,
Soft and pulling,
Slithers through the reeds
Like a mocassin

And slides your boat
From its mooring.

Returned now
You sit below the bank,
Flinging ivory pebbles
Into the dark quietness

At the arched mouth
Of the moon.

SALMON POINT

All afternoon the sun stuck to our backs
As we climbed the logging trails
Up the high white meadows to timberline.
Now only ten minutes of light hang on the shrubs
As we sit here at the edge of Salmon Point.
Below us two ravens swoop over the spruce,
And quietly drop into the night
Seeping up from the gullies.
A bank of fog is sliding in from the south,
And soon it should hide the village lights
Spread across the valley.
Far to the west we see this continent
Break into coastline,
Splintering off into islands that rise
Like loaded haywagons in a deep green field,
Islands anchored like old frigates
Waiting for a flicker of light from Salmon Point.
We must now fire a deep red beacon,
Telling our beaches are long, wet and empty.

SNOW-CLOUDS

Tonight the snow bristles off Verstovia's back
And builds into cold winter thunderheads,
The dust from shaggy palominoes
Stampeding down to graze in the low-country.
It seems the sky is blazing with white ridge fires.
Squalls of tribes are sweeping
From their sanctuaries in the uplands--
Clouds of owls, a flock of wet swans
Coming down to forage outside the window.

FRANKENSTEIN

Everything must have a beginning, to speak in Sanchean phrase; and that beginning must be linked to something that went before.
Mary Shelley

O, hideous doll.
My dark, dim-witted lake.

You are a continent pulled
From a dream,
A land that lies still
And unmapped--
In you I pour my own pulse,
And stitch a wind
That blows your heart open
Like a door.

I teach you
Only to fear fire,
To survive on all that I give.
O, son.
My hideous echo--
I whisper of ice,
Of sleeping mastodons

And tbe sounds of fossils
Crawling out of place.

GODDARD HOT SPRINGS

The hot springs start in the hills,
Trickling through a vent,
Up through the earth's door--
A haze bubbling from the ground,
Its breath--roots steaming under the ferns,
Sliding like veins of mercury.
When you lie in the sweating streams
You are lying in the breath of your ancestors,
The old pioneers who came north
And sat in the pools,
Mapping trails to the mother lode.
You feel a fog drift through your body,
A voice that is strangely familiar
And still has stories to tell.

TRANSCANADIAN

At this speed, my friend, our origins are groundless.
We are nearing the eve of a great festival,
The festival of wind.
Already you can see this road weakening.
Soon it will breathe
And lift away to dry its feathers in the air.
On both sides the fields of rape seed and sunflowers
Are revolting against their rows.
Soon they will scatter wildly like pheasants.
Now is the time, my friend, to test our souls.
We must let them forage for themselves,
But first--unbuckle your skin.
It is out here, in the darkness
Between two shimmering cities,
That we have, perhaps for the last time, chance
Neither to be shut nor open,
But to let our souls speak and carry our bodies like capes.

THE CASCA

Though the decks are warped,
The hull split and
Stowed with fireweed,
The Casca's bell still
Clangs in the wind;

It calls me out
Over the alder flats,
Drawing me closer
Until its sound
Pounds like the pulse
Of the riotous miners

Who float from beneath
The giant paddle,
And lure me
Into the luminous dark,
Undercurrent of the dead.

ECLIPSE

Father
I have come back
To this squat Minnesota town

This shrinking house
These bald fall rooms
To find you in a stack

Of dim photos
Curled like leaves
In the back of a drawer

I run my thumb
Over your face
And feel the glassy

Bristles of your mustache
The creases
Along your cheeks

I roam your eyes
I always
Find you laughing

We stare at each other
And I feel you
Lose your gloss

You draw me downward
Page by page
Photo by photo

Until your body is warm
And massive and my hand
Loses itself in yours

We stand on Sorin's Bluff
And watch the wind
Die in the elms

Our shadows melt
Into one another
As we squint

Through two worn negatives
At the moon sliding
Across the sun

The valley darkens
And I am left blind
Until the sun jumps

And catches the trees
Until the moon
And you father fade

And leave me
Holding these cold
Exposures

This reverse bond
From which I pull myself
Head-first

To grip the first
Warm object
I see

HART CRANE ALONG THE MISSISSIPPI

with a line from Rimbaud

I am the scholar of the dark armchair,
And sitting alone here late at night
I watch the hills fold one by one into themselves.
The lights of the village on the far shore rise
And glow like a low constellation,
And the nighthawks dive and trill like tree toads.
I am the scholar of the dark armchair.
I am the poet, king-seaman.
Around my head mayflies swing their sweet death-flutes.
And I hear them sing: you are the scholar of the dark armchair.
Moths hover over my hands, and glide to the moons
Rising in the pools of my palms,
Singing: you are the scholar of the dark armchair.
You are the poet, king-seaman.
And feeling the tug of the seaweed,
I walk to the shore
And wait for the sails of the Orizaba.
I wait for death's moist wings to dry on the sand.
I wait for a pale breeze that always flows south,
Calling: I am the scholar of the dark armchair.
I am the poet, king-seaman.
I am the poet, king-seaman.

HERMITAGE

If you follow this path back,
You come to a clearing
Where the grass is dark and delicate,
A place where the earth is so damp
It is like stepping
Into something coolly interior

A region whose borders
Are defined only by desire,
A land where one longs to go unshaven,
Where doors open one by one
And the wicks of the skunk flower
Burn all night over the shallow pools.

MOUNTAIN ASH

In winter when I walk
Home after dark,
I hear a wind
Catch the mountain ash.

I watch it move
Through the branches,
Rattling
The berries still

Clinging to the tree.
They look to me
Like flames,
The kind you see hanging

In cabin windows--
Red pearls,
Bulbs of sparks
Blown over the snow

Until only the wind
And I are left:
Two men conversing,
Yet not one word uttered.

HARBOR AT MIDNIGHT

On these docks I walk in one world,
Yet stare down into another whose moon
Moves through the water like a jellyfish.
I dive into its side, and find
This world rocks quiet and civilized.
A soft wind sings in the riggings of its trawlers.
I watch for lanterns burning in the cabins,
I hear only voices, and smell the smell
Of fishermen pressing close.
Suddenly I am blinded by the pulse of matches.
And voices ask what sea my smooth features are from,
Why I am beardless and wet?
They ask if my body moves with the seaweed,
And feels the pull of the tides?
They ask if my voice sings like the wind?
They ask if my veins carry their currents?
I stand silent, and stare back simple as a fish.

AND THE MOUNTAINS BEHIND (for Carolyn)

On this bit of sand we stand and stare seaward. Aside from the night, there is no motion--no shoal lights, no gulls, no small curlews flashing over the sea's back. And even the sea itself lies calmed. It stretches long and wide. It stretches purple. And like the night, we have come to be woven by its shadow. We listen and have no fears. We feel the air stir at our backs. And we know the mountains behind are turning fluid, and like the night ready to surge down around us.

SITKA SPRUCE

1.

I swear these trees come from before,
Dumb stragglers from the edge.
In their trunks the fossil worm still sings.
In the shade of each branch
There are crickets still barking like sea lions.
Legends tell of main veins shooting
Deep into the earth
To feed off pools of red lava,
That some run South along the fault lines,
Churning through coastal bays and inlets--
And when a Latin peasant clears his land
The cutting and crackling of roots
Is felt here, far North
Where a tree will shiver and shed one cone.

2.

My wife and I watch the orphan trunks
Ride with the tides back to the land.
They roll and slide like whales,
Their smooth brown backs flashing in the sun.
We have seen them drifting in the Bering,
Following the songs of seals--
Uncut totems beautifully round and faceless,
Waiting for the masks of ancient clans
To rise, and chant again like the winds
That draw the foam from the sea.

3.

I have heard that when we die
These spruce will take and mother the moon.
We will find it nestled among the roots,
In a crowd of friends,
A child with a quarter face.
Stepping forward it will offer us
A gift wrapped in moss--
A pale cone out of which we pick the sharpest teeth,
And opening our hands we prick our palms,
And watch as the first seeds of blood
Trickle and combine into pools,
Rich seas the roots curl and slide for.

ISADORA

quotations from The Art of the Dance
by Isadora Duncan

Kyrie kyrie say yes to Isadora
Say yes say yes to madame Dolorosa
Say yes to Walt Whitman yes to Yesenin
Say yes say yes kyrie kyrie

"Often when people have questioned my morals, I have answered that I consider myself extremely moral because in all my relations I have only made movements which seem beautiful to me."

Tonight Isadora beauty is home
And if beauty is home then I sleep
I send my arms deep into its darkness
Tracing along its cool wet paths
Through fogs that rise and swirl
Curling like your scarves past my hands
Because Isadora beauty is home
And if beauty is home then I sleep
And moving deeper I see you rise
Stand and dance your scarves
You let your body shine pale
Because Isadora tonight beauty is home
And if beauty is home then I sleep
I feel the sweep of your gown
I breathe with your hair
I ride the currents of your lungs
I swim with your hands
Because Isadora beauty is your home
And if beauty is your home then I sleep

"Of all movement which gives us delight and satisfies the soul's sense of movement, that of the waves of the sea seems to me the finest. This great wave movement runs through all Nature."

And tonight Isadora the waves run long
I feel their inner lifts and falls
And in turn receive your dance your loves
And I name you Whitman my Yesenin
And say yes because Isadora the waves run long
I watch your white arabesque
Crest with each live swell
I watch your scarves move out across the sand
I watch your pulse drive and dance over the rocks
And I hear the dark cup your purple flecks of light
And the tide running long says

Kyrie kyrie say yes to Isadora
Say yes say yes to madame Dolorosa
Say yes to Walt Whitman yes to Yesenin
Say yes say yes kyrie kyrie

watching valentino

cutting the room
in two frames

the light wavers
past her shadow

and spreads valentino
over the ripples
in the sheet

our laughter
hides in the click
of the reels

as the great lover
slashes his way
through the ruins

and sweeps
vilma banky
onto his stallion

they slowly
disappear
against the dunes

we lower the sheet
from the wall

and spend the night
on its sand

INSTINCT

It's all in the way
We pass
The blind man in the grocery.

It's that last twitch
That brings us
Awake as we lie half-dreaming
Against the sofa.

It is you,
Hard part of the brain,
Tiny pebble picked from my shoe
After a walk--
When all else fails
I come back
And call you 'brother' of my eyes.

In the mornings
At the mirror
It is you I see on four legs,
Your voice I hear
Scratching like a dog
At the door.

And at night
When my wife and I
Lie quiet,
And the wind is through the trees,
I pass you on
Into her.

I come to you now weak
And freezing
And offer you a mole
And call it my first cousin.

I call you Sixth Finger,
Last Match--
And tell you you're the stanza
I've waited my whole life to write.

UMBRA

The moon supposed to be not touched. No one suppose to go there.
Dominic Charlie,
Capilano Indian

The moon takes root
In this fallen cairn

This ancient altar
At the top of the ridge.

Lured by its light
Between the stones

I wander down
The inner staircase

Through bones
And scrolled maps

Through artless gods
Half eaten away.

I pass through
Tunnels and caves

Over mounds of hides
And wooden knives;

Drawn by the moon
To the quiet light

Into its camp
Of shaggy nomads.

They circle and
Squat like boulders

Graze the roundness
Of my head.

They smell the blossoms
Of my ears

And lift and pull
My tongue to watch it

Slip like a fish
Through their hands.

They whisper to my feet
The invention of my name.

ROBERT HEDIN was born in 1949 in Minnesota. He was graduated from University of Alaska and presently lives in Sitka, Alaska where he teaches literature and writing at Sheldon Jackson College.

1000 copies of SNOW COUNTRY have been letterpressed at COPPERHEAD on 75 lb Sonora text from Tree Swenson's handset New Times Roman type purchased from Mackenzie & Harris, San Francisco, who imported the mats from England. The trade edition was perfect bound by Northwest Bookbinding, Portland.

40 copies, letterpressed on 80 lb Carousel text, have been handbound in quarter leather with handmade hand-marbled papers and hand-stitched headbands by Annie & John Hansen. Each has been numbered and signed by the poet.

Special thanks to Centrum Foundation, Fort Worden State Park, Port Townsend, Washington, where Copper Canyon Press is Press-in-Residence.